LET'S TALK ABOUT SUMMER

INTERNATIONAL POEMS

Edited by Gino Leineweber

Verlag Expeditionen

Publisher: Verlag Expeditionen
Edited by Gino Leineweber, 2017
Let's talk about Summer
International Poems

Cover-Photo and Design: Birgitta Sjöblom
Depicted is the "Installation Nomade" of French artist Guy
Lorgeret ("Open Art 2015", Örebro / Sweden)
Title: Dalia Staponkutė

ISBN 978-3-943863-75-8

If it could only be like this always—always summer,
always alone, the fruit always ripe...
Evelyn Waugh

Table of Contents

Table of Contents

PROLOGUE

Rhodes in Greece is not only a wonderful island for the citizens and visitors, but also for art.

You can see it in various places. One of them is the International Writers and Translators Center in Rhodes City, which was established in 1996 together with the Three Seas Writers' and Translators' Council (TSWTC) under the auspices of UNESCO. The TSWTC represents writers and translators of the countries around the Aegean , the Baltic and the Black Sea – in a word, the 'three seas', whose members undertook a remarkable cruise in the Black Sea two years earlier.

The result of the journey was the 'Delphi Declaration' followed by the Center and Council. The latter, with about 30 members from 17 countries located around the 'three seas', brings writers, translators, and events to Rhodes.

After the last General Assembly of the TSWTC in May 2017, the secretary, Dalia Staponkute, a writer from Lithuania and the president, Gino Leineweber a poet and writer from Germany, visited the Art-Garden in Afandou in Rhodes, Greece. During their stay, they happened , together with the owner , Damon Papakiriakou, to think about extending the common visual - arts exhibitions to include poetry.

Considered a good idea, poets from all over the world were asked to contribute one of their poems in English as well as in their mother tongue.

The topic of the poems was *Summer*. The result was 37 poems from Bosnia and Herzegovina, Cyprus, Georgia, Germany, Greece, India, Italy, the Netherlands, Poland, Rhodes, Romania, Spain, Turkey, the United Kingdom, the United States and Uruguay.

The TSWTC committee not only decided to feature this wonderful collection in the beautiful ArtGarden in Rhodes, but also to make a chapbook out of the thoughts and pictures of these poets about summer. We address all lovers of poetry and hope you, the reader, will enjoy the poems of the exhibition in Rhodes. It is a unique occasion to have such an international selection.

Gino Leineweber
Editor and
President of the TSWTC

THE MEADOW
Alison Townsend, USA

> *"Often I am permitted to return to a meadow"*
> *—Robert Duncan*

We all go there eventually,
taken by the dark god from the green
meadow life must seem as one is departing
toward another meadow, where it is always
night, though we like to think
(don't we?) that there is something
light there, if only glow-in-the-dark
stars the god has painted or pasted
on the ceiling of that world
so that something about the place
where we will reside forever seems
a bit like home. That is, if the soul
has a home without the body. Sweet
body, that rots or burns behind us,
body it is hard to imagine – as I sit
in this bright room, sun warming
my hand as it moves across the page –
ever being without. As if the soul
were smoke or a wisp of fog, something
we can't contain, that moves over
the meadow, touching everything lightly,
weaving itself into every strand
of grass, though we'd like to pin it down.
Life is a story about the soul, after all,
unfashionable as that sounds, hard
as it is to say in the twenty-first

century with the force and solemnity
it deserves, repeating the word soul
the way Sappho said, lyre, lyre, lyre,
the words dancing together on a scrap
of parchment like music,
fragments meant to be memorized
even as they are sung.

A BOTTLE OF JEAN NATÉ
Alison Townsend, USA

"...the mysteries emerge from the private and even secret
world of female experience..."
—Helen Foley, The Homeric Hymn to Demeter

My mother smelled like this
when I was a girl, though I must twist
the cap on the bottle I bought at Walgreen's
to remember the lemony amber, suspended
in woody florals she'd splash over her body
after a bath, laughing, repeating the ad
that urged women of the early 60's to
"tingle at the touch of Jean Naté"
and "glow from head to toe."

She did glow then, the way the living do,
as she lay in the bath tub, stretching
a long leg to turn the hot water faucet
with her toes, no cancer yet, her small,
blue-veined breasts high and firm,
covered shyly with a washcloth
when she caught me looking, studying
the map of who I might become,
so I could understand what it meant.

I sat there, on the closed lid
of the commode, playing with the black
velvet ribbon around the bottle's neck,
sneaking glances at the mysterious
world of her body, talking about things
I cannot remember. Though my body does,
and precisely – those summer afternoons

she stood beside me, wrapped in a Turkish
towel, splashing cologne the color
of Pernod or celadon across her neck and arms,
then splashing me, dabbing a bit behind
my ears, the cool, green scent
rising around us in a cloud – tingling,
glowing, the body's private story
hidden but not quite gone.

SUMMER
Anna Nasiłowska, Poland

summer shines
and heats and smells
and thrives and dances
and sings and nourishes
and give water and rushes
and lie down and spends
too much and give for free
and admires themselves
and promises
o, promises
always too much

LATO
Anna Nasiłowska, Poland

lato świeci
i grzeje i pachnie
i kwitnie i tańczy
i śpiewa i karmi
i poi i pędzi
i przysypia i wydaje
za dużo i rozdaje darmo
i zachłystuje się sobą
i obiecuje
o, obiecuje
zawsze ponad stan

SUMMER'S END
Anna Würth, Germany

A breeze of frangipani
twilight hour blues
the cicada silent

TIMELESS

No calendar
for the tides of love
diving through the foam

LOVESTONED
Translated by John Waterfield, United Kingdom

Honey seized by surprise
the dance
whips us together
more spice was never
hair-fine hip-wide
in a passing touch
pliantly plucked in flight

SOMMERABSCHIED
Anna Würth, Deutschland

Frangipaniluft
Blaue Stunde bluesgegerbt
Stumm die Zikade

TIMELESS

Keinen Kalender
für Gezeiten der Liebe
tauchen in die Gischt

LIEBESTRUNKEN

Honig im Handstreich
peitscht uns der Tanz
zusammen
mehr Pfeffer war nie
haarscharf hüftbreit daneben
schmiegsam
sich rupfen im Flug

THE HOUSE OF AROMAS
Annabel Villar, Uruguay/Spain

... to my grandmother, "who wins"

Suddenly, the days became longer
and summer broke out impetuous,
with its blue and orange sky
and the smell of broom, grapevines and saltpeter.

Silent, the House of Aromas waits for me
with the aroma of jasmine and aged calmness,
in this Sunday of remembrance
only my mother and the friendly ghosts coexist.

I rebuild my life traveling through the pictures
and I traverse history inside drawers and ward-
robes.
I discover that I have been happy,
that bad hours swept away from my head the blissful
ones,
but despite everything, they are there,
waiting hiddeng while I learn to uncover them.

They invite me to open my senses to the past,
bring me out from the pictures
to the light and life outside,
to return among wisterias
to the childhood of bread and quince,
at the place of happiness
where my grandmother reigned.

Absorb again the scents that caress like hands,

*hear anew how onions crackled in the oil
and smell vinegar and fragrant Februarys
which permeated the grapevines of her yard.
And glued once again to her heels,
hear the rustle of starch at her hips
and the creak of wood under her steps,
firm and strong.*

*And in the nights feel once more
the smell of the iron warming up
my sheets and my memories.
And leaning back on her chest
sink again into her fragrance
of forget-me-nots, basil
and spearmint.*

LA CASA DE LOS AROMAS
Annabel Villar, Uruguay/España

> *... a mi abuela, "la que vence".*

Súbitamente,
los días se hicieron más largos
y el estío irrumpió impetuoso,
con su cielo azul y naranja
y el aroma de las retamas,
las parras y el salitre.

Silenciosa,
la Casa de los Aromas me espera
con olor a jazmines y antigua parsimonia.
En este domingo de remembranzas,
sólo conviven en ella mi madre
y los fantasmas amistosos.

Reconstruyo mi vida viajando por las fotos
y recorro la historia por cajones y armarios.
Descubro que he sido feliz,
que las malas horas barrieron
de mi cabeza a las dichosas,
pero a pesar de todo ahí están,
confiando agazapadas
mientras aprendo a descubrirlas.

Ellas me invitan a abrir mis sentidos al pasado,
sacarme de las fotos a la luz
y a la vida de allí afuera, para volver entre glicinas
a la infancia de pan y de membrillo,
al lugar de ser feliz donde reinaba mi abuela.

Embeberme de nuevo en los aromas
que acariciaban como manos,
oír de nuevo a la cebolla crepitar
en el aceite y oler el vinagre
y los fragantes febreros
que impregnaban las parras de su patio.

Y pegada otra vez a sus talones,
escuchar el frufrú del almidón
de sus caderas y el crujido de las tablas
bajo sus pasos, firmes y fuertes.

Y en las noches sentir una vez más
el olor a plancha entibiando
mis sábanas y mis recuerdos.
Y recostándome en su pecho
volver a hundirme en su fragancia
de nomeolvides, albahaca y hierbabuena.

PARTHENIAS
(A summer's dream)
Barry Stevenson, United Kingdom

Shy, master of the boldest, subtlest lines
and hide from fame
down alleyways and in the backs of shops,
drinking with slaves –
I'm at your back crouched like a thief hiding
much like yourself.

Fame is the spur that wings you. Stealth is all.
You edge backwards
and I tap you on the shoulder, so.
You start and stare.
I bow and dare to tell you of my thing.
You look relieved
then clap your hands. A hundred sparrows rise
into the air

– there's your poem, you say, then disappear.

LAUGHTER
Barry Stevenson, United Kingdom

Thracian Tereus, Procne's man,
raped her sister Philomel ;
and that she might not of this tell,
cut out her tongue.
Undaunted, Philomel told her woe:
a web the muted victim wove
and sent it to her sister so
that she should know.
Now Procne read this terrible thing
and killed her first-born, Itys,
and served him to her lord and king,
there at Daulis.

There at Daulis,
he found out and he went spare.
He chased the sisters miles and miles
up hills, down dales, he knew not where.
Which unkindness
moved the gods to make them birds, lest
in their running wrong and blindness
worse befall them in their great distress.

We hear them still:
Tereus is the fisher king,
Procne a swallow on the wing
and Philomel's a nightingale,
whose summer song can never fail.

NOTHINGNESS HE IS
Betül Tariman, Turkey
Translated: Osman Yener

torn; what was he to me
the man I meticulously raised
defeated and naive, as if in a prayer

the more I stitch up, the more the tent of tediousness
expands
the surmise that I smeared on my hand
sweating like a horse running over hurdles
bad-tempered and too few

torn; the narrowness that upsets
it is me the woman who upsets me
i am paralyzed, I have no hands
what if I lean my forehead to my chest

dreams do not rain on the house of the poor

HİÇLİK O
Betül Tariman / Türkiye

yırtık; neyimdi ki o benim
itinayla büyüttüğüm erkek
dua eder gibi çocuksu yenik

diktikçe genişliyor sıkıntı çadırı
büyüyor elime sıvaştırdığım zan
engelli koşuda terlemiş
at kadar huysuz ve az

yırtık; can sıkan darlık
o benim beni üzen kadın
felçli ve ellerim yok
alnımı göğsüme dayasam

yoksullar evine düş yağmaz ki

KUNILINGUA
Bogdan Baran, Poland

Good night to your eyelids closed
By the seal of my foreign tongue
Dry is the night from rustle of words
The last drop of speech still swaying

How do we find in abysses of grammars
The proper word humid like a sea
How do we meet in the morning
After the sleepless labyrinth of flection

You are the flower and I am your name

NAKROPOLIS
Bogdan Baran, Poland

Deities flown down from here long ago with squeal
of seagulls
Women dressed and undressed to drown finally in
the cloud
Forgotten wind blew away from cracks the rem-
nants of time
Calmness grows with the morning heat and it will
be so here forever

We walk the hill like in thousand years
I make you photo and send it out into cosmos
When it returns we'll be eternally
Free from the speech like that acropolis meadow

KUNILINGUA
Bogdan Baran, Polska

Dobrej nocy twoim powiekom zamkniętym
Pieczęcią mojego obcego języka
Sucha jest noc od szelestu słów
Jeszcze się kołysze ostatnia kropla mowy

Jak odnajdziemy w przepaściach gramatyk
Właściwe słowo wilgotne jak morze
Czy się natkniemy na siebie rano
Po nieprzespanym labiryncie fleksji

Ty jesteś kwiatem a ja twoją nazwą

NAKROPOLIS
Bogdan Baran, Polska

Bóstwa dawno temu sfrunęły stąd w dół z piskiem
mew
Kobiety rozbierały się i ubierały aż utonęły w chmu-
rze
Zapomniany wiatr wywiał ze szczelin resztki czasu
Cisza rośnie od rana z upałem i tak tu już zawsze
będzie

Idziemy wzgórzem jak za tysiąc lat
Robię ci zdjęcie i wysyłam w kosmos
Kiedy powróci będziemy już wiecznie
Wolni od mowy jak ta łąka akropolu

EVERY GARDEN A PLACE OF WORSHIP
Christine Geweke, Germany
Translation: Benjamin Geweke, Germany

grasses, they sway in the urban space
swaying long since before mankind
head to wind, singing grass blades, delicate
panicles, driven into restless sparkling

on the outskirts the air untamed, bird-manly
a moai in the fields ejects the evil spirits
the long ears have long ceased to listen
every garden worshipped in the sun oven

JEDER GARTEN EINE KULTSTÄTTE
Christine Geweke, Deutschland

süßgräser, sie wiegen sich im urbanen raum
wiegten sich schon lange vor den menschen
im wind. singende grashalme, filigrane
rispen, die im getriebensein haltlos funkeln

am stadtrand die luft ungezähmt. vogelmännlich
ein moai im grünen die bösen geister vertreibt
die langohren hören schon lang nichts mehr | jeder
garten eine kultstätte im erdofen der sonne

MOMENTS
Deborah D'Agostino, Italy
Translation Helen Guyatt - United Kingdom

Glimmers of Sunlight paint the vineyards
and scattered houses form colourful herds.
Foggy was the day
like a heavy cloak
covering the clouds
in the airless Immensity that strokes the earth.
The heavy heart,
filled with tears,
oppresses the soul.
Painful silence of summer sultriness
and turns the heart to images
imprinted on the memory,
to the immense valley of childhood dreams
...and the farmer finishes
another bale of hay...
and everywhere the scent of acacia,
the scent of a short summer lie.
Only a moment the illusion of the past,
then the sudden return
to the wastelands, without hope,
opening into the real world
beyond the windows of the heart.

ATTIMI
Deborah D'Agostino - Italia

Spiragli di Sole dipingono le vigne
e le case sparse formano greggi colorate.
Fumoso il giorno
come se una cappa
pesasse le nuvole a mezzo levate
nell'Immensità rarefatta che sfiora le terre.
Il cuore spugnoso,
imbevuto di lacrime,
grava l'anima.
Silenzio pensoso d'afa estiva
e torna il cuore alle immagini
impresse nella memoria,
all'immensa vallata dei sogni d'infanzia
...e completa il contadino
un'altra balla (di fieno)...
e ovunque odore d'acacie,
l'odore della breve bugia estiva.
Solo un attimo l'illusione del passato
per tornare d'improvviso
nelle lande chiare, senza speranze,
che apre il mondo reale
oltre le finestre del cuore.

MAN
Dorel Cosma, Romania

*Overpowering pain
slides on the dark sky
and the white veiled string
punctuates the sea
of resignation.
Deep suffering
with tense fingers
pointing tot he terrible nail
piercing the flesh.
On the cross,
abandoned in his pain,
Man.
And the groan of simple weeping
of the instant fact,
with life and its current
value.
in the cold emptiness of pain,
ordeals locked away.
Frightful respect
There
hangs
HE
and YOU
may now demand from yourself.*

OMUL
Dorel Cosma, Romania

Covârşitoarea durere
alunecă pe întunecatul cer
şi firul alb voalat
străpunge marea resemnării.
Suferinţă adâncă
cu degete crispate
spre înfiorătorul cui
ce carnea o străpunge.
Pe cruce,
părăsit durerii sale,
Omul.
Şi geamătul cu plânsul simplu
al clipei fapt,
cu viaţa în valoarea sa
circulatorie.
În golul rece al durerii,
în chinuri zvârcolite.
respectul temător.
Acolo
unde atârnă
EL
ca TU
să ştii să ceri şi de la tine.

THİNKİNG OF YOU
Emel Kaya, Cyprus
Translation: Gürgenç Kormazel, Cyprus

*A man and I, we pass from under the strawberry
soufle
flux of soufle, a pair of Syrian eyes,
tramway 47 passes the heap of the noise*

*as if escaping outside but shrinking inwards
red bloods cells pass from the nape of my neck
a sparrow song, the summer of 95, only a little fur-
ther*

*the tramway rushes over my step, over my hipbone
the soufle is stale, the rails piercing, this tittle-tattle,
the nausea
the retine says ah oh, bitter is the coffee after meat-
balls and bean salad*

you can't cross the road sometimes

SENİ DÜŞÜNMEK
Emel Kaya, Kıbrıslı

geçiyoruz çilekli sufle altından benle bir adam
Suriyeli bi' çift göz, akıntısı suflenin,
47 nolu tramvay geçiyor ses yığınını

dışarılara kaçar gibi içerilere büzülen
alyuvarlar huzmesi geçiyor ense kökümden
serçe merçe ötüşü, '995 yazı, iki arpa boyu

hızla geçiyor tramvay adımımın üstünden, leğen
kemiğimden
sufle bayat, geçiyor beni delip raylar, gevezelik,
bulantı
ah oh geçiyor retina, köfte piyaz üstüne kahvenin
acı tadı

insan karşıdan karşıya geçemiyor bazen

YESTERDAY
Emina Kamber
Translation: Gino Leineweber from German version

Yesterday
You
Trimmed
My
Flowering Path
And
Decorated
My
Hair
With
Lilies
Today
You pulled the thorns
Out of my wounds
That
Stung me
On your way
I am
Alive

DO JUČER
Emina Čabaravdić-Kamber

Do jučer
Si moj cvijetni put
Njegovao
I
Moju
Kosu
Sa
Lilijama
Kitio
Danas
Izvlačis trnje
Iz mojih rana
Na koje
Sam se
Na tebi
Određenom putu
Nabadala
Ipak
Ja živim

DAYDREAMS OF JUNE
Funda Aytüre, Turkey
Translation: Mesut Şenol, Turkey

*Heavenly touch. the sin of the trees. the lament of
the lampions. the divine hymn played by the bells.
Incensed days. we used to have velvet dreams. that
voice spellbound me.
that endless aria. your filtered sunny eyes. your
heart is twenty-four carats.*

*1. The tale of humanity starts with love
    My heart bundles you up
2. The foam of love rides on the wings of the night
    What is left for us is a sacred condemnation
3. The sound of the snow is embedded in the night
and your eyes the incense of the days
    The flower gets hurt
    While the ballad of the leaf
    Was being sung in unknown climates
4. As the crucified loves proliferate in the world
    The loneliness gets crowned beyond the fences
    Humanity becomes estranged from its essence
    If it does not get out of its dark cave
5. Without love humans become dirty
    While there is an ongoing rose slaughtering in
life
6. The pain becomes deeper on our face
    My poetry is an orphan child
    In the night when you mention about me
7. I loved you with the beauty
    Of the never aging spring seasons*

8. I'd be crippled by bends in my particular times
  The threads thicken where the fingers get thinner
9. The words feel ashamed
  As the migratory birds leave
10. For some reason the trains make me feel odd
  A strange love rolls inside me
11. The glasses are left half empty which were pre-
sented
  By the years
  Is it the way to write love stories accompanied
by the rain

  Which daydream happens to be the lie of a heart
  If only I would have been a lullaby for a child's
spirit

HAZİRAN DÜŞLERİ
Funda Aytüre, Türkiye

Tanrısal dokunuş. günahı ağaçların. kandillerin
ağıtı. çanların söylediği ilahi şarkı.
Tütsülenmiş günler. kadife düşlerimiz vardı. o ses
büyüledi beni.
o sonsuz arya. süzme güneş gözlerin. yirmi dört
ayar yürek seninki.

1. Aşkla başlar insanlığın öyküsü
   Sarıp sarmalar yüreğim seni
2. Gecenin kanatlarında aşkın köpüğü
   Kusal mahkumiyettir hesabımıza düşen
3. Gecede kar sesi gözlerin günlerin tütsüsü
   İncinir çiçek
   Bilinmeyen iklimlerde söylenirken
   Yaprağın türküsü
4. Çarmıha gerilen sevdalar çoğalırken dünyada
   Çitlerin ardında taçlanır yalnızlıklar
   Özüne yabancılaşır insan
   Çıkamazsa karanlık mağarasından
5. Aşksız kirlenir insanlar
   Gül kıyımı sürerken yaşamda
6. Acı katmerlenir yüzlerimizde
   Yetim bir çocuktur şiirim
   Beni anmadığın akşamlarda
7. Seni eskimeyen baharların
   Güzelliği ile sevdim
8. Vurgunlar yerim tikel zamanlarımda
   Parmakların inceldiği yerde çoğalır ipler
9. Sözcükler utanır
   Göçmen kuşlar giderken

10. Nedense trenler beni bir hoş eder
Salınır içimde garip bir sevda
11. Yılların sunduğu yarım bırakılmış
Kadehler
Yağmurla mı başlanır aşk öyküleri yazılmaya

Hangi düş yalanıdır bir yüreğin
Çocuk yüreğine ninni olaydım

SUMMER DAY
Gino Leineweber, Germany

Sun and sand and sea
White sails on the water

I am laying flat on my belly
And feel
The silence in the universe

Falling backwards in the sky

Suddenly
Somebody is calling someone
A girl laughs

The sun
Reflecting
On her soaking hair

SOMMERTAG
Gino Leineweber, Deutschland

Sand und See und Sonne
Auf dem Wasser weiße Segel

Ich liege auf dem Bauch
und spüre
die Stille im Unendlichen

Rückwärts falle ich ins All

Dann ruft
irgendjemand irgendwen
Ein Mädchen lacht

Auf seinem nassen Haar
spiegelt sich die Sonne

THE LAND OF MULBERRY
Gonca Özmen, Turkey
Translator: Ruth Christie, United Kingdom

Come to the land of mulberry
To the remoteness of dwellings

I'll teach you quiet
And the branches' concern

I'll kiss where you're waning
Where nature wanes

Cross the plain
Come to the land of mulberry
Into the grasses

I'll make you listen to the storm
To the scream of the storm-god

A long while later
I'll wait for you again
Beyond a stream

Cross the field
Come closer come
To the mulberry scent

I'll show you the ants

DUTLUK
Gonca Özmen, Türkiye

Dutluğa doğru gel
Evlerin uzağına

Sana susmayı öğreteceğim
Dalların kaygısını da

Azaldığın yerden öpeceğim
Azaldığı yerden doğanın

Ovayı geç
Dutluğa doğru gel
Arasına otların

Sana fırtınayı dinleteceğim
Theşub'un çığlığını

Bir suyun ardında seni
Neden sonra yine bekleyeceğim

Tarlayı geç
Daha gel daha
Dut kokusuna

Sana karıncaları göstereceğim

BLACK PURSE
Gurinder Singh Kalsi, India

*I don't know
How many times
I took the purse out of my pocket*

*I don't   know
How much money
I spent from it.*

*I saved and spent
Thousands of rupees*

*It kept carefully
 Many postal stamps*

*My I card
My identification
My loose papers
Addresses of my friends*

*A long piece of time has passed
I don't know
How many days
How many months
How many years*

*But, today,
I remembered suddenly
That this black leather purse
You bought for me
With a great love*

When it got into my mind
I shivered
And the black leather purse
Also shivered

The non-living black, leather purse
Came to know
The language of love.

SEPTEMBER
Haydar Ergülen, Turkey
Translation: Mesut Şenol, Turkey

Woman goes away and this accounts for poetry
woman goes away and out of this a poet comes into life
(I know of which woman makes me a poet)
If "it is told everywhere that the summer is over" (*)
woman's departure is spoken of all over
pronounced everywhere as a poem wherever the woman
goes:
Woman's going means the end of the summer, far and
wide
the summer finishes when the woman disappears, paving
way to poetry,
end of the summer becomes poetry; poetry means the end
of love...
If only the city with its districts would go after the sum-
mer
the summer becomes longer and that brings benefits to
loves
the city after the summer, poetry after the woman
One goes to September's district like this
in one night I went to September from June
September was left by the summer so was poetry by June
it was deserted by the woman for that fable;
All sons leave the mom for a poem!
Should that woman walk out on me then I become a poet
the woman to whom I am her son, do not dare to forsake
me,
it is only a poem uttered, a summer ends, and a woman
goes

All women leave poetry to be replaced by a woman!

EYLÜL
Haydar Ergülen, Türkiye

Kadın gider ve bunun şiir olduğu söylenir
kadın gider ve bir şair doğar bundan
(Ben hangi kadından şair olduğumu bilirim)
"Yazın bittiği her yerde söylenir"se (*)
kadının gittiği de her yerde söylenir
kadın gittiği her yerde şiir diye söylenir:
Kadının gittiği yazın bittiğidir, her yerde
yaz biter kadın giderse, bunun sonu şiirdir,
yazın sonu şiirdir, şiirdir aşkın sonu...
Şehir her semtiyle yazın peşine düşse
yaz uzar bundan ve aşklar da nasiplenir,
yazın peşinde şehir, kadının peşinde şiir
Eylülün semtine kadar böyle gidilir
bir gecede gittimdi Hazirandan Eylüle
Eylül yazdan terkedilmişti, şiirse Haziranda
kadın tarafından terkedildi o söylenceye:
Bütün oğullar anneyi bir şiire terk eder!
O kadın beni terk ederse şair olurum
oğul olduğum kadın sakın beni terk etme,
şiirdir söylenir, yazdır biter, kadındır gider

Bütün kadınlar şiiri bir kadına terk eder!

SUMMER RAIN
Hilal Karahan, Turkey

*Looking for a place to go back
Became a stranger wherever it went
An umbrella left in the train
Few words spoken to side seat
Yet it didn't know wherever to go
carrying itself within*

*The harbours sulked so much that
eyes burnt by the fire
of the fairy tales it believed
Looking for a place to go back
real journeys were returnings
Yet it didn't know that it was to seek
and go overflowing boundaries*

*It had to rush to collect its hands
time was moving
It was an illusion, a pouring
body to obscure the meaning
Yet it knew that to be understood
was the most dangerous thing
Holding its heart in the hand*

YAZ YAĞMURU
Hilal Karahan, Türkiye

dönebileceği bir yer arıyordu
hangi şehre gitse yabancı
trende unutulmuş şemsiye
yan koltuktakiyle iki kelime
bilmiyordu ki nereye gitse
kendini de yanında taşıyordu

fena küsmüştü limanlar
gözlerini yakıyordu ateşiyle
kavrulduğu masallar
dönebileceği bir yer arıyordu
dönüşlerdi gerçek yolculuklar
bilmiyordu ki aramak
ve gitmekti yükümlü olduğu
sınırlarından taşıyordu

çabuk toplamalıydı ellerini
zaman kımıldanıyordu
bir illüzyondu, dökülüyordu bedeni
anlamı gizliyordu
biliyordu ki anlaşılmak
en büyük tehlikeydi
yüreğini elinde tutuyordu

HOUSE OF PIES, AUGUST 1972
Holly Iglesias, United States

Peach crumb, Dutch apple, Queen Anne cherry, strawberry rhubarb, Derby pecan, coconut custard, black bottom, French silk, banana cream, all rotating in glass cases, mesmerizing, as we sat at the counter, hungry for a piece of something sweet and uncomplicated, grateful for ice water to wash down Wallace and Watergate before leaving the country for good. The man I had just married studied me like the instructions to a simple machine, hoping to assemble una vida americana of his own, and though he abandoned the project almost before it began, he did learn how to sit in a diner like he belonged there, to tap his cup gently for a refill, to tip the waitress extra if she winked, sliding him a slice of lemon meringue, pastel as a cloud over Cuba.

*FATHER, WON'T YOU CARRY ME, CARRY ME,
CARRY ME*
Holly Iglesias, United States

The first time I saw the Mississippi from the air, I knew my place, and I knew that home was a sinuous ribbon lacing east to west, past to future, bondage to possibility, appearing and disappearing like a snake in new-mown hay as the sun flashed on its surface. I have crossed many times the bridge that takes me home then takes me away, by car, by train, and even on foot, the current electric beneath me as St. Louis crouches on the western bank like a weary roustabout. Each spring the river swells there, rolls out of its ancient bed to sweep away all that is dead or forgotten, all that is foolish or weak, the debris tumbling inevitably south—spinet and spire, cottonwood and calf.

INFANTICIDE
Juan C. Tajes, Uruguay/Netherlands

A child is killed, will not reach young,
a young man is killed, will not reach adult,
humanity is debased, future weakens.
They will not be parents, mothers,
they will stop being children, brothers,
they will become rotten flesh, wormy.
For that, they do not serve the philosophy of others
nor the quotation given.
In that instant the privilege ceases,
non-commitment.
The pretense of trivializing reality
in the name of lofty ideals
higher thoughts, abstract metaphors.
While the bombs fall and the poets are silent,
while cheering the score and are silenced dead,
while the notion of homeland
change of sphere and what matters
it's not that the world turns but a ball
so something smells rotten on the planet
and intelligence delights
in the common dunghill of collective memory.
Resigned to kill and die like beasts
licking between the carrion.
And the bombs fall, children die,
the party continues
poets sing to prostitute muses
by derision, by complacency.
This is not justice, this is not courage.
Only hate, revenge and shame.
And not even that.

INFANTICIDIO
Juan C. Tajes, Uruguay/Nederland

Se mata a un niño, no llegará a joven
se mata a un joven, no llegará a adulto
se envilece la humanidad, se debilita el futuro.
No serán padres, madres,
dejarán de ser hijos, hermanos
se volverán carne putrefacta, agusanada.
Para eso no sirven la filosofía ajena
ni la cita prestada.
En ese instante cesan el privilegio,
el no compromiso,
la pretención de banalizar la realidad
en nombre del elevados ideales
pensamientos superiores, metáforas abstractas.
Mientras las bombas caen y los poetas callan
mientras se aclaman goles y se silencian muertos
mientras la noción de patria
cambia de esfera
y lo que importa no es que el mundo gire
pero que una pelota emboque
entonces
algo huele a podrido en el planeta
y la inteligencia se regodea
en el estercolero común de la memoria colectiva.
Resignados a matar y a morir como bestias
relamiéndose entre la carroña.
Y las bombas caen, los niños mueren,
la fiesta sigue, los poetas cantan
a prosituidas musas
por el escarnio, por la autocomplasencia.
No hay justicia, no hay coraje.
Sólo odio, venganza y vergüenza.
Y ni siquiera eso.

HOW FRAGILE BEAUTY IS TONIGHT...
Julio Pavanetti, Uruguay/Spain
Translator:
María Juliana Villafañe, Puerto Rico/USA

How fragile beauty is tonight
suspended between candid remains
braided with the fiber of summer
that converts your body into an ocean.

Untangled from the shadows, the moon
moves between whitened ants
and lays to dream among us
with the soft murmur of waves.

Accomplice of the games in the dark
disperses over the ocean the seeds of light
particles of a mysterious dust
that the breeze entangles in your hair.

The sand remains warm
delineates the contour of our bodies
while your hands reinvent filigrees
to the bird that poses in my back.

Your lips slide through the steps
in my flesh, advances without obstacles
crosses the hallway of my essence
and makes my wings unfold.

QUÉ FRÁGIL LA BELLEZA DE ESTA NOCHE...
Julio Pavanetti, Uruguay / España

Qué frágil la belleza de esta noche,
suspendida entre cándidos resquicios
trenzados con la fibra del verano
que convierte en océano tu cuerpo.

Desprendida de las sombras, la luna
se desplaza entre hormigas blanquecinas
y se tiende a soñar, junto a nosotros,
con el arrullo suave de las olas.

Cómplice de los juegos en lo oscuro,
dispersa sobre el mar luz en semillas,
partículas de polvo misterioso
que la brisa enmaraña en tu cabello.

La arena permanece aún caliente,
delinea el contorno de los cuerpos,
tus manos le reinventan filigranas
al pájaro que vuela por mi espalda.

Tu boca se desliza por la grada
de mi carne, y avanza sin obstáculos,
atraviesa el pasillo de mi esencia,
y logra que mis alas se desplieguen.

RAFFAELLO CECCOLI'S ICON, 1853
Liana Sakelliou, Greece

My father liked the icon.
I was alive, he was not a painter.
"Only this lasts," he used to whisper.
He held me tightly in his arms
like Ceccoli must have held his easel.
But where was the fountain?
In the lion's mouth?
In the courtyard, beyond the tombs?
Deep in the plane trees' shadows?

I wanted the spring in the open
so his palm with the
unbroken lifeline
would always be there
behind the painting.

Η ΕΙΚΟΝΑ ΤΟΥ ΡΑΦΑΗΛ ΤΣΕΚΟΛΙ, 1853
Λιάνα Σακελλίου, Ελλάδα

Στὸν πατέρα μου ἄρεσε ἡ εἰκόνα της.
Ήμουν ζωντανή, δὲν ἦταν ζωγράφος.
Μόνο αὐτὴ διαρκεῖ, μοῦ ψιθύριζε.
Μὲ κρατοῦσε στὴν ἀγκαλιά του σφιχτὰ
ὅπως ὁ Τσέκολι τὸ καβαλέτο.

Διακρίνεις τὴν κρυμμένη πηγή;
Μέσα στὸ στόμα τοῦ λιονταριοῦ;
Στὸ προαύλιο, δίπλα στοὺς τάφους;
Ἴσως βαθιὰ στὰ πλατάνια;

Διάλεξα τὴν πηγὴ ὑπαίθρια
ἀφοῦ ἡ παλάμη του μὲ τὴν
ἀτάραχη γραμμὴ τῆς ζωῆς
θὰ κρυβόταν πάντα
πίσω ἀπ' τὸν πίνακα.

VACANCE D' ETE, 2016
Lily Exarchopoulou, Greece

Promenade des Anglais:
Unalloyed scars
during the Bastille extravaganza

Early morning jogging
late evening running
midnight clubbing
The inhabitants must be
extraordinarily fit

Worked out muscles
Do not prevent Death.

The tourists are pretty happy

Joy does not exclude the Assumption

Undead mortals
Watch the living
From the Purgatory

Hate erodes their stubs
Pain their figures
Stampede their relaxation

Hashed are the speechless Niçois

They at least know
Paradise does not live here anymore
Mohamed and Jesus withhold it
on the grounds it hurts.

ΚΑΛΟΚΑΙΡΙΝΕΣ ΔΙΑΚΟΠΕΣ, 2016
Λίλυ Εξαρχοπούλου, Ελλάδα

Αμιγής μαχαιριά
η Promenade Anglais
στην εξτραβαγκάνζα της Βαστίλλης

Πρωινό τζόγκιγκ
βραδυνό τρεχαλητό
μεταμεσονύκτια διασκέδαση
Οι κάτοικοι είναι
εξαιρετικά γυμνασμένοι

Οι μύες δεν εμποδίζουν
τον θάνατο.

Οι τουρίστες πολύ ευχαριστημένοι

Η χαρά δεν εξοβελίζει την Κοίμηση

Απέθαντοι οι πεθαμένοι
παρακολουθούν τους ζωντανούς
από το Καθαρτήριο

Το μίσος διαβρώνει τις ουλές τους
Ο πόνος τις μορφές τους
Το ποδοβολητό την ηρεμία τους

Σιωπούν ανίκητοι οι Νικαίοι

Τουλάχιστον αυτοί γνωρίζουν
Πως ο/η Παράδεισος
δεν είναι πια εδώ
Μωάμεθ και Ιησούς τον αποκρύπτουν
καθότι πονάει

MY FIVE ELEMENTS ARE SACRED
Lipi Da Mahandev, India

I am not saying this in the context
That I am the best man for centuries
Or from all creatures

This is my first and last life

Not because
I could not have love
But because
I love the girl
Who has no father.

PAINTING
Meenu Sukhman, India

I paint my day
Draw a line of hope
My tolerance is my eraser
I color my painting with love and patience
I complete it with a final touch
of my sweet smile
It will be finished with the call of God
I go on filling colors
And thank God.

JAPANESE GARDEN
Maren Schönfeld, Germany
Translation: Klaus-Dieter Wirth, Germany

Japanese garden
between paving stones
a molehill

Discussing a poem
at the edge oft he pond
a bathing blackbird

JAPANGARTEN
Maren Schönfeld, Deutschland

*Japangarten
zwischen Schieferplatten
ein Maulwurfshügel*

*Gedichtbesprechung
am Gartenteichufer
badet eine Amsel*

*LET THE EYELASHES OF THE SUMMER BRUSH
YOUR EYES*
Mesut Şenol, Turkey

*with the sweats
of the wheat fields
another world would've opened
longing
painting the canvas yellow
the chant from the heart
was charmed with the words
the storm in the inner world
of the deserting person without a backward glance
setting accounts with the moments
already passed and ended
screams
at the summer movie theatre
the fireflies
the guardians
of the flaming pale blue air
a request
starting with me
and ending with me
ah, go figure
and find a cure for me
let your making love with your essence go
let the eyelashes of the summer
brush your eyes*

YAZIN KIRPIKLERI DOKUNSUN GÖZLERINE
Mesut Şenol, Türkiye

bir öte alem açılırdı
buğday tarlalarının
terleriyle
tuvali sarıya boyayan
hasret
sözlerle kamaştı
bir yürek teranesi
ardına bakmadan terk edenin
iç dünyasındaki fırtına
geçen ve biten
anlarla hesaplaşma
yaz sinemasında
çığlıklar
ateşböcekleri soluk mavi
yalaz havanın
bekçileri
benimle başlayan
ve biten
bir maruzat
ah gel de çare
bul bana
bırak özünle sevişmeyi
yazın kirpikleri
dokunsun
gözlerine

WEAVE OF COLORS
Nurduran Duman, Turkey
Translation: Andrew Wessesl, United States

caught every morning in the lover's hair, the sunset
circulates through its strands of red, of light

because every arrow emerges from the dawn
evening is weaved from midday to joy
from sorrow to night... an opposite, a face

everyone knows sharing is sacred
if leaves and statements don't decay, then death
is a green garden, its reward infinite

people evaporate from boiling water to the face of
the sky
painting the sky blue so it rains
the person who plants the growing tree is mixed
with the infinite

there are people who love rain and also those who
don't know how to love

RENKLERIN ÖRGÜSÜ
Nurduran Duman, Türkiye

âşık her sabah saçlarında günbatımı
dolaşır saçaklarına kırmızının, ışığın

tan yerinden çıktı diye her ok
örülür akşam öğleden sevince
hüzünden geceye… bir ters bir yüz

herkes bilir ki paylaşmak kutsaldır
ölüm yeşil bir bahçe ödülü sonsuz
yaprak ve söz çürümesin tek

kaynar sulardan buharlaşıp göğün yüzüne
mavi çalanlar var, ki yağsın
ağaç diken de sonsuza karıp kendini

yağmuru seven de var bilmeyen de sevmeyi

THE SKY SETTLED ON THE LAKE
Nurduran Duman, Turkey
Translation: Andrew Wessesl, United States

the sky settled on the lake, clouds a flying carpet
we prepare to step on the moon, its walk
and pass over the moon's dance, its water and time

rustling hydrogen skirts float
passing by our sides by our heads. daybreak.
we spread and are spread from cinnamon to blue
from diamond from bee
we're graced with fields and gardens on the earth's
silk

we, too, are learning to cultivate: its light

GÖK YERLEŞMIŞ GÖLE
Nurduran Duman, Türkiye

gök yerleşmiş göle, bulutlar uçan halı
adımladık adımlıyoruz ayı, yürüyüşünü
üstünden geçiyoruz dansının, suyla zamanın

uçuşarak hidrojen etekleri süzülüyor
yanımızdan başımızdan. tan.
saçıp saçılarak tarçından maviye elmastan arıdan
tarlalar bahçeler beziyoruz yerin ipeğine

öğreniyoruz biz de ekip biçmeyi: ışığı

HAMBURG SUMMER ...
... OF EMANCIPATION
Reimer Boy Eilers, Germany

Waves are glittering
Over the pontoon
Into my white corner

On the pretty
Lake Alster
Only women
Take their turn

Men are smiling
From astern

HAMBURGER SOMMER ...
... DER EMANZIPATION
Reimer Boy Eilers, Deutschland

Wellen glitzern
Übern Ponton
In mein weißes Eck

Auf der schönen
Alster segeln
Nur noch Frauen

Männer lächeln
Her vom Heck

SONG FOR MY NEIGHBOR
Ruhsan İskifoğlu, Cyprus

my neighbor's old toilet set
moribund blinds are always on the terrace

My neighbor talking of good things
Its song scares at living room

tv channel and even the radio is on
when no one is at home

neighbor balcony yell regularly everyday
natured doormat to trap himself
to its strange emptiness

KOMŞUM İÇİN ŞARKI
Ruhsan İskifoğlu, Kıbrıslı

komuşumun eskiyen tuvalet takımı
can çekişen güneşlikleri hep terasta

iyi şeyler anlatıyor komşum
şarkıları ürkütüyor oturma odasında

evde kimse yokken çalışır
televizyon kanalları, hatta radyosu

balkonu hergün düzenli bağırır
huylu paspası hapseder kendini
garip boşluğuna

THROUGH THE COMBS OF AUGUST
Suleiman Alayiali-Tsialik, Rhodes, Greece

Through the combs of August
as the sun sets piously
igniting his last wildfire
let dreams and desires kindle
to the challenge of the light
where the sea patiently trains
and the rocks look smaller during the summers,
I meditate in the bright twilights.

On the waterfront of the harbor town I grew up
I now lie on a different raft
and my body breaks at a right angle
as a sign utterly irreversible defying the fire
slow to catch the flame like yarrow
with bell peals narrating the past
of a beloved coast - a crucible of the centuries -

Always with the vision of the fire
- perpendicular at first, then crawling
ever more closely licking the horizon -
how heavy a burden becomes nostalgia.

The splendid sea, how deeply we have injured her!

And while Echo hides herself in her rocky cave
with the hopeful tiptoeing of her time,
the pointers on the heavenly clock slowly grow ru-
by-red
darkening the caress on the faces of the lilies -
and how to measure the truths of life with precision.
Thus simply a new space intervenes
a consoling silverer between sea and land
and an ideal trainer for those who cast away the
shield of dreams
where they may be better taught the details
by the inexhaustible chapter of emotion.

But the sea, the sea…

ΜΕΣΑ ΑΠ' ΤΑ ΧΤΕΝΙΑ ΤΟΥ ΑΥΓΟΥΣΤΟΥ

Σουλεϊμάν Αλάγιαλη-Τσιαλίκ, Ρόδος, Ελλάδα

*Μεσα απ' τα χτενια του αυγουστου
καθώς ευλαβικά γέρνει ο ήλιος
ανάβοντας την τελευταία του πυρκαγιά
να φουντώσουν τα όνειρα κι οι πόθοι
στην αναμέτρησή τους με το φως
εκεί που η θάλασσα γυμνάζεται με υπομονή
και λιγοστεύουν οι βράχοι τα καλοκαίρια,
διαλογίζομαι σε δειλινά ευήλια.*

*Στην προκυμαία του λιμανιού που μεγάλωσα
ξαπλώνω σε μιαν άλλη τώρα σχεδία
και ορθή το κορμί μου διασπάται γωνία
σα σήμα διόλου αντιστρεπτό που δε φοβάται τη
φωτιά
σα χόρτο το μυριόφυλλο που αργεί να ντουμανιάσει
με κωδωνοκρουσίες που ιστορούν τα περασμένα
ενός γιαλού αγαπημένου - χωνευτήρι των αιώνων -*

*Πάντα μετά την οπτασία της φωτιάς
- κατακόρυφη στην αρχή κι έπειτα έρπουσα
 τον ορίζοντα ολοένα λείχοντας -
τι πάθος δυσβάσταχτο που γίνεται η νοσταλγία.*

Την πανώρια θάλασσα πόσο την επληγώσαμε.

Κι ως η Ηχώ κρύφτηκε στη βραχοσπηλιά της
με αισιόδοξα του καιρού ακροπατήματα,
σιγορουμπινίζουν οι δείχτες στο ρολόι τ' ουρανού
σκουραίνοντας το χάδι στις όψεις των κρίνων
και πως μ' ακρίβεια να μετρηθούν της ζωής οι
αλήθειες.
Ένας νέος χώρος έτσι απλά παρεμβάλλεται
ασημωτής παρήγορος ανάμεσα στη θάλασσα και τη
στεριά
και ιδανικός εκπαιδευτής για ριψάσπιδες ονείρων
όπου τις λεπτομέρειες πιότερο μπορούν να διδαχτούν
απ' της συγκίνησης τ' απύθμενο κεφάλαιο.

Όμως τη θάλασσα τη θάλασσα...

TODAY AND TOMORROW
Surjit Singh Jeet, India

Today
What I am
I may not be the same
Tomorrow
And what in store
Will tomorrow have for me
I don't know
So I
Tell myself
Not to worry
Not to hurry
As today is passing by
On its own accord
And
Patting me to sleep
Only if it happens to be
To wake up
In an ever new
Tomorrow.

GOOD DAYS
Tarsem, India

My hands are in your hands.
Your hands are in my hands.

When the hands
will be greeting
each other
Then you will be me
And I will be you
Then no one can stop
The good days to come .

A DISAPPOINTED THOUGHT
Tariel Chanturia, Georgia
Translation: Manana Dumbadze, Georgia

A poem needs a heart. A poem needs a liver.
A poem needs a tear, and plenty of your blood.
A poem needs a leg. A poem needs a hand.
A poem needs a brain and a forehead as well.
A poem needs dollars. Rubles are also needed.
True poetry needs sex. And a poem comes next.
A poem needs fury. A poem needs a fist.
A poem needs Barbie for a granddaughter's
smile,
A poem needs wine, fruits and vitamins as well.
Plenty of sleepless nights and time to time a
nap.
A poem needs anger. A poem needs poison.
Centuries (a lot), and a couple of seconds.
Surely, at night - surely, at noon,
Devotion of somebody's, devotion of yours.
A poem needs poetry. A poem needs candies.
A poem needs honesty.
A poem needs cedar. A poem needs oak.
A poem needs a heart and a bullet in that heart.
A poem needs a mountain. A poem needs valley.
A poem needs a wife (sometimes a second wife).
A poem needs a breast and a dagger through
that breast.A long and quiet sleep, and a dead
mom's lullaby - so sweet.

*A poem needs sheep and a shepherd for that
sheep.*

I do know what a poem needs.
Have no idea, who needs a poem?

იმედგაცრუებული ფიქრი

ტარიელ ჭანტურია, საქართველო

ლექსს ჭირდება გული. ლექსს
ჭირდება ღვიძლი.
ლექსს ჭირდება ცრემლი. ლექსს
ჭირდება სისხლი.
ლექსს ჭირდება ფეხი. ლექსს ჭირდება
ხელი.
ლექსს ჭირდება მკერდი. ლექსს
ჭირდება წელი.
ლექსს ჭირდება ტვინი. ლექსს
ჭირდება შუბლი.
ლექსს ჭირდება ლარი. ლექსს
ჭირდება რუბლი.
ლექსს ჭირდება სექსი, თუ მართლაა
ლექსი.
ლექსს ჭირდება რისხვით აღეული
წარბი.
შვილიშვილებისთვის ლექსს ჭირდება
ბარბი.
ლექსს ჭირდება ღვინო. ლექსს
ჭირდება ხილი.
უძილობა ბევრი, ცოტა-ცოტა ძილი.
ლექსს ჭირდება მუშტი. ლექსს
ჭირდება შხამი.
საუკუნე ბევრი, სამი-ოთხი წამი.
რა თქმა უნდა ღამით, რა თქმა უნდა
დღისით,
ერთგულება შენი, ერთგულება მისი.
ლექსს ჭირდება ფიცი. ლექსს ჭირდება
ლექსი.

ლექსს ჭირდება ტორტი. ლექსს
ჭირდება კექსი.
ლექსს ჭირდება დეკა. ლექსს ჭირდება
ხვია.
ლექსს ჭირდება მკერდი და იმ
მკერდში ტყვია.
ლექსს ჭირდება ქედი, ლექსს ჭირდება
მოლი
ლექსს ჭირდება ცოლი (ხან მეორე
ცოლი).
ლექსს ჭირდება მკერდში გარჭობილი
დანა.
დაქინება მერე და მკვდარ დედის ნანა.
ლექსს ჭირდება ცხვარი და იმ
ცხვრისთვის მწყემსი.

ეს არ ვიცი ოლონდ, ვის ჭირდება
ლექსი.

THIS SUMMER
Uwe Friesel, Germany

This
summer
is heavy
The days
swell
Spawn is glued to the roofs
The rainy sky
leaks through

The hips of the women are edgy
whereas the men
speak
in copious words

Down
at the lake
birds rip feathers
off each other

DIESER SOMMER
Uwe Friesel, Deutschland

Dieser
Sommer
ist schwer
die Tage
blähen sich
Laich
klebt an den Dächern
der Himmel
läßt Regen durch
Die Hüften der Frauen sind eckig
während die Männer
Weitläufiges
sagen
Unten
am See
rupfen die Vögel einander Federn aus

*OLEVANO ROMANO – MY PARADIES FOR
THIRTEEN WONDERFUL YEARS*
Uwe Friesel, Germany

*Since two days, the sun is roaring once again from
the ski. Where yesterday evening veritable cataracts
were foaming, this forenoon the age-old staircases
made of soap stone bridle away, as if it never had
been otherwise.*
*Before long, drinking water gets scarce. It is now
portioned by the quarters, at times here, at other
times there, for no more than two hours.*
*As in every summer? No, not quite. A change lies in
the air, first by mouth propaganda, then per public
advertising. During the next days, water counters
should be installed in every household.*
*A crying shame! Soon we'll have to pay for the air
we breath!*
*The pool-owners complain about the injustice of the
uniform water levies and point at the car washers,
who earn money with the common good. In turn, the
car washers accuse those who water profusely their
flowers and terraces. Should not they be the first to
end the waste? And with a sweeping gesture, you
are informed that practically all Olevanese consume
far too much of the precious water, with the excep-
tion of the one standing in front of you.*
*The notion that there is an Italian, a European,
meanwhile even a global water-problem seems so
far-fetched that at this point, every discussion dwin-
dles to zero.*

OLEVANO ROMANO – MEIN PARADIES FÜR
DREIZEHN WUNDERBARE JAHRE
Uwe Friesel, Deutschland

*Seit zwei Tagen brüllt die Sonne wieder vom Him-
mel. Wo eben noch Katarakte geschäumt hatten,
bröseln die Treppen aus Speckstein vor sich hin, als
sei es nie anders gewesen. Nicht lange, und das
Trinkwasser wird knapp. Es wird quartierweise
zugeteilt, mal hier, mal dort für je zwei Stunden, wie
jeden Sommer. Das heißt, nicht ganz wie jeden
Sommer. Eine Änderung kündigt sich an, zunächst
per Mundpropaganda, dann per Plakatanschlag:
Künftig soll das Wasser nach Verbrauch bezahlt
werden. In den nächsten Wochen würden überall
Zähler eingebaut.*
*Ein himmelschreiendes Unrecht! Bald werden wir
sogar die Luft bezahlen müssen, die wir atmen!
Schon beklagen die Swimmingpool□Eigner die
Ungerechtigkeit des Einheitstarifs und verweisen
auf die Autowäscher, die damit Geld verdienen, die
wiederum auf jene, die ihre Blumen und Terrassen
mit dem kostbaren Leitungswasser wässern. Sollen
doch die erst einmal Schluss machen mit ihrer
Verschwendung! Und mit einer ausladenden Arm-
bewegung wird dir klargemacht, wie alle übrigen
Olevanesen mit dem Wasser aasen, nur dein
Gegenüber nicht.*
*Dass es ein gesamtitalienisches, gesamteuropäisch-
es, ja inzwischen auch ein globales Wasserproblem
gibt, kommt ihm derart abstrakt vor, daß an dieser
Stelle jegliche Diskussion ins Stocken gerät.*

REFUGEES
Yiorgos Chouliaras, Greek
Translated by the author and David Mason, United
States

On the other side
of the photograph I write to remind myself
not where and when but who

I am not in the photograph

They left us nothing
to take with us
Only this photograph

If you turn it over you will see me

Is that you in the photograph, they ask me
I don't know what to tell you

ΠΡΟΣΦΥΓΕΣ
Γιώργος Χουλιάρας, ελληνικά

Από την άλλη πλευρά
της φωτογραφίας γράφω για να θυμάμαι
όχι το πού και πότε αλλά ποιος

Δεν είμαι εγώ στη φωτογραφία

Τίποτε δεν μας άφησαν
να πάρουμε μαζί μας
Μόνον αυτή τη φωτογραφία

Αν τη γυρίσετε από την άλλη θα με δείτε

Εσύ είσαι στη φωτογραφία, με ρωτούν
Δεν ξέρω τι να σας πω

SAMADHI - THE SHADOW OF SUMMER
Zorin Diaconescu, Romania

*We assume, based on their missing clothes
that Adam and Eve lived in perpetual summer
while in Paradise; winter was therefore a later discovery
in the post-edenic world?
The cold missing, spring and autumn do not make any
sense either -
nor do clothes or any other aspect of what we call com-
fort.
So, what was, after all, life in Paradise like?
We don't know, neither do the priests,
as all concerns go to what happened later, because
we should, so we are told, strive to return,
save our undying soul, get back to where our ancestors
were driven from,
but what it is like to live forever,
well, nobody's got a clue.
Nihil sine deo is an almighty password,
beware! It tells me, all we do, whenever and whatever,
we act
in the name of God. Obey!, or confront all who believe,
become an outcast,
not welcome at their table. I wonder, this is what the
Lord told us? This is how we are supposed
to please Him? Find our way back? Back to what? (By
the way, how do we know it's "him"?)
On the other hand, don't worry, everybody's gonna die
anyway,
meanwhile we're free to choose between 'have to' and
'want to'
and what happens if I want nothing? Of course, nobody
has to answer this question.*

SAMADHI – UMBRA VERII
Zorin Diaconescu, Romania

Presupunem, pe baza absenţei hainelor
că Adam şi Eva au trăit într-o vară continuă
In timp ce se aflau în rai; iarna e aşadar o descoperire
ulterioară
în lumea post-edenică?
În absenţa frigului primăvara şi toamne nu au sens -
nici hainele sau orice alt aspect pe care îl numim confort.
Aşadar, cum era de fapt raiul? Nu ştim, nici noi nici
popii,
toată atenţia e îndreptată spre ce s-a întâmplat după,
deoarece
am fost informaţi, trebuie să luptăm, să ne întoarcem,
să salvăm sufletele noastre nemuritoare, să ne întoarcem
acolo de unde au fost alungaţi strămoşii,
dar cum e să trăieşti veşnic, ei bine, nimeni nu are habar.
Nihil sine deo e o parolă foarte puternică, bagă de
seamă! Tot ce facem,
oricând şi oriunde, facem În numele lui Dumnezeu.
Acceptă!, sau ţine-le piept credincioşilor, pregăteşte-te
de haiducie,
nu vei fi binevenit la masa lor.
Mă întreb, asta ne-a transmis
Dumnezeu? Asta aşteaptă el de la noi? Calea de întoar-
cere? La ce anume?
(De fapt, de unde ştim că e "el")
Pe de altă parte nu vă bateţi capul, oricum murim,
între timp suntem liberi să alegem între 'trebuie' şi
'vreau'
ce se întâmplă daca nu vreau nimic? Desigur, nimeni nu
e obligat să răspundă.

SHORT BIOGRAPHIES OF THE POETS

Alison Townsend's newest book is *The Persistence of Rivers: An Essay on Moving Water*, winner of the Jeanne Leiby Prose Award. She is also author of two award-winning books of poetry, *Persephone in America* and *The Blue Dress*, and two chapbooks. Her writing appears widely, and awards include a Pushcart Prize, a literary fellowship from the Wisconsin Arts Board, the Crab Orchard Open Poetry Competition Prize and the University of Wisconsin-Whitewater's Chancellor's Regional Literary Award. Professor Emerita of English at the University of Wisconsin-Whitewater, she lives in the farm country outside Madison. She has recently completed *Nature Girl*, a collection of interrelated essays.

Anna Nasiłowska published her first poems in 1977; now she is a professor of Polish literature, writer and poet. She has written novels and essays; also biographies of the couple Jean-Paul Sartre and Simone de Beauvoir, of mainly Polish poetess Maria Pawlikowska - Jasnorzewska and of Ryochu and Yoshiho Umeda, two Japanese living in Poland.
She loves traveling, she's visited Latin America, Japan and Africa, but she loves Greece the most.
Anna Nasiłowska is active in many fields. She was elected President of the Association of Polish Writers in 2017.

Anna Würth's poems and short stories have been published in 74 anthologies and in her book *Aphrodite.Lovestoned* by Wachholtz. In 2001 she received the Literary Sponsorship Award GEDOK. She regularly gives public readings both in Germany and abroad. In her new *Literary Pictures* the author and photographic artist combines her poems with her photography. They were exhibited in Paphos, Cyprus, quite recently in 2017.

Translator: Dr John Waterfield, London. Doctorate in classics and English literature at Christ Church, Oxford. He has worked as a music instructor in the UK and Germany.

Translation of Rainer Marie Rilke's *The Duino Elegies,* E. Mellen Press, 1999.

Author of: *The Heart of His Mystery: Shakespeare and the Catholic Faith in England under Elizabeth and James,* I Universe, 2009.

Annabel Villar is a poetess and cultural activist. Founder and Treasurer of "Liceo Poético de Benidorm", C.E.D.R.O., REMES, Movimiento Poetas del Mundo (Uruguay), Northamerican Academy of Modern Literature and World Poetry Movement (WPM).

3rd Poetry Award in IV Contest of Poetry "Traspasando Fronteras", University of Almería, Spain, 2010. Great East-West Arts Award, International Academy Orient-Occident, XVI International Festival "Poetry Nights", Curtea de Arges, Romania, 2012. Own publication: *Viaje al Sur del Sur* (Ed. Germanía, 2015)

Betül Tarıman is a Turkish poet and essayist. She studied History at Hacettepe University. Her first poem appeared in Kıyı magazine in 1992. Other magazines that have included her work are Varlık, Gösteri, Sözcükler, E Edebiyet, Damar, Yasakmeyve, Adam Sanat and Edebiyet ve Eleştiri. She was the recipient of the Necatigil Poetry Prize in 2005. She currently writes literary ads and essays for Cumhuriyet Kitap.

Bogdan Baran – Polish writer and essayist, author of several literary and philosophical books and nearly a hundred translations in the realm of humanities and literature from German, English, French, Italian and Russian. He graduated in philosophy and mathematics at <u>the Jagiellonian University</u> (Cracow, Poland). He earned a doctorate for his dissertation on Martin Heidegger and Emmanuel Levinas. Member of the <u>PEN-Club</u>, member of the Board of the <u>Polish Writers' Association</u>, chairman of the Board of the Literature House in Warsaw.

Christine Geweke is a painter, sculptures and lyricist. She is a member of the Hamburger Autorenvereinigung e. V. (Hamburg Writers Association) and heads the art room for lyric, paintings and sculptures. On 8.3.2009 she launched the "Charta der SchriftstellerInnen für die Wahrung des Weltfriedens" ('Charta of authors for preserving world peace') and has started publishing anthologies with peace as the theme. Published volumes of poetry: *Engeltanz* (*Angel Dance*) , 2005, *venediglich T* (*Venetian T*) , 2011, *Abriss* (*Demolition*) , 2012, *augen blick doppel klick* (*blink of an eye double click*) , 2015 and *ein jahr hautnah* (*one year up close*) , 2016.

Deborah D'Agostino is a poetess, writer, cultural promoter and lives in Rome (Italy), where for the past twenty years she has been an organizer and presenter of cultural events. Has published poetry collections: *Gabbiani d'asfalto* (2006 Ed. Lampi di Stampa) and *Spezza le catene* (2007, Ed. Arduino Sacco). Winner of numerous national and international prizes for her poetry published in anthologies, magazines and art catalogues. Presents creative writing laboratories in the Italian schools and literary meetings. Member of "BPW Italy", founder of Cultural Association "Crescere Insieme".
Translator: Helen Guyatt (Oxford) has trained as a scientist, with a PhD in epidemiology and 100 scientific publications in tropical medicine and public health. She lived in Umbria (Italy) for 10 years, raising four children and establishing an olive farm. She now lives in Kenya and works in the monitoring and evaluation of humanitarian relief programs.

DOREL COSMA, Romania, holds a B.A. in Journalism, radio-tv producer, senior editor of several newspapers and magazines, chairman of the I.G.F. World Folklore Union, manager of the Palace of Culture, the most important cultural institution of his hometown. Author of several books published in Romania, Bulgaria, Italy, Greece, Egypt, France, Argentina, Germany, Austria, Spain and the U.S.A., among which: *Flight* (poems), *Malul Tăcerii, La*

Rive du Silence (*The Shores of Silence*, poems), *Në kopshtin e kohës, În grădina timpului* (*In the Garden of Time*, poems), *The Shores of Silence, Sessizligin Kiyisinda, Malul Tăcerii* (poems), *Duminica în Manhattan* (*Sunday in Manhattan*, essays), *Biletul de călătorie* (*The Ticket for Eve*r, poems).

Emel Kaya completed postgraduate studies on the language and terminology of medical texts in Ottoman Turkish in 2002 and PhD studies in the same field in 2008 at Selcuk University, Turkey. Her poems and essays on language and literature have been published in various literary magazines. She was the organizer and the moderator of the Iskele International Poetry Festival (in Cyprus) in 2013-2016. Her poems have been translated into English, Greek and Persian.

Emina Kamber is a poetess, painter and a teacher of exile literature and art, born in Kakanj, Bosnia-Herzegovina and living in Hamburg, Germany since 1968. She is deputy chairwoman of the German Writers Union (VS) in Hamburg, a member of the German Exile PEN VS. In 1988 she established the international Literature Club „La Bohemina".
Emina Kamber has published books in different languages and received various Literature Awards.

Funda Aytüre is a Turkish poetess. Beside poetry she has written essays, diaries, letters and short stories. She is also involved in painting and music. She is the author and composer of some musical pieces.

Her play, called *Forgive me World* , was staged in Antakya. Her poems and prose writings have appeared in literary magazines, newspapers and anthologies such as Evrensel Kültür Güzel Yazılar, Damar, İtaki, Şiir Odası, Yazılıkaya, Ünlem, and Beşparmak. She is the recipient of several awards.

Gino Leineweber has been active as a poet since 1998. From 2003 to 2008 he was editor / editor in chief of the *Buddhist Monthly Magazine* (*Buddhistische Monatsblätter*). He has three poetry books published so far and poems in international anthologies and magazines.
From 2003 to 2015 he was Chairman of the Writers' Association Hamburg (Hamburger Autorenvereinigung); thereafter Honorary Chairman.
Since 2013 he has been President of the Three Seas Writers' and Translators' Council (TSWTC) based in Rhodes, Greece.

Gonca Özmen studied English language and literature at the University of Istanbul. She received her M.A. degree in 2008 and her Ph.D. degree in 2016 from the same department. She has been writing poetry, essays and reviews in several literature magazines and newspapers since 1997. Her first poetry book *Kuytumda* (*In My Nook*) was published in 2000 and her second book, *Belki Sessiz* (*Maybe Silent*) was published in 2008. She has been awarded several poetry prizes. Her poetry collection, *The Sea Within* (Selected Poems, translated by George Messo) was published by Shearsman Books in February 2011.

Translator: Ruth Christie is a freelance translator of Turkish. She studied English language and literature at the University of St. Andrews. She taught for two years in Turkey and later studied Turkish language and literature at London University. With Saliha Paker, she translated a Turkish novel by Latife Tekin (Marion Boyars, 1993) and, in collaboration with Richard McKane, a selection of the poems of Oktay Rifat (Rockingham Press, 1993), a major collection of Nazım Hikmet's poetry (Anvil Press, 2002) and a collection of Bejan Matur's poetry (*In the Temple of a Patient God*, Arc Visible, 2004).

Gurinder Singh Kalsi is a poet and storywriter. He has 17 books to his credit. He is a National Award winning writer. His writings are about life and nature. He also writes for children. By profession he is a science teacher in a government school. He is also a good painter.

Haydar Ergulen is one of the important poets of the present generation in contemporary Turkish literature. He graduated from the Sociology Department at Orta Doğu Teknik Üniversitesi (Middle East Technical University) in Ankara. Among his published poetry books are: *Sokak Prensesi* (*Street Princess*/1991), *Eskiden Terzi* (*Once a Tailor*), *40 Şiir ve Bir* (*40 Poems and One*/1997), *Karton Valiz* (*Cardboard Suitcase*/1999). With *40 Poems and One,* Ergulen won the prestigious 1997 Behçet Necatigil Poetry Award as well as the Orhon Murat Arıburna Poetry Award . His *Once a Tailor* brought

him the 1996 Halil Kocagoz Poetry Award .
He has used the pen name 'Hafiz' in some of his
books.

Hilal Karahan is a Turkish poetess, writer, transla-
tor, mother and medical doctor. Her professional
poems, stories, interviews and articles about poetry
have been published in various national and interna-
tional poetry-culture-literature magazines since
2000. She has participated in many collective books,
bilingual poetry almanacs and organizational com-
mittees of international poetry festivals. Her poems
and selected poetry books have been translated into
many languages. She has 6 poems, 2 essays, and
many selected poem books in various languages.
She is a member of Turkish PEN and intercontinen-
tal director of World Festival of Poetry and Writers
Capital Foundation networks.

Holly Iglesias' work includes two collections of
poetry—*Angles of Approach* (White Pine Press) and
Souvenirs of a Shrunken World (Kore Press)—and
Boxing Inside the Box: Women's Prose Poetry
(Quale Press). *Sleeping Things*, her most recent
poetry collection, is forthcoming from New Rivers
Press. She has received fellowships from the Na-
tional Endowment for the Arts, the North Carolina
Arts Council, the Edward Albee Foundation, and the
Massachusetts Cultural Council.

Juan C. Tajes, Montevideo. Multidisciplinary art-
ist, & drama teacher, communicator, teacher of ora-
tory art at the University of Sciences Politiques de

Paris. Edited work (excerpt): Poetry: *Canto al Hombre* -1963 / *Cristos de arcilla* -1964/1965 / *Tantango* - Magazine of the National Tango Academy of Buenos Aires - 1996 / *Time of words* -2016 / Anthologies: *Folder Vanguard* (Anthology) - 1963/1965 / *Sonetos*- Magazine *De tweede ronde* - Amsterdam / Tale: *The other war* / Paris / *The dead and the metaphor / The great silence of Ramadí / El Crímen / Nemesis or the miracle / Manual de cuhilleros* / Theater: *Amicitia 83* / Essay: *Art and society / Jorge Enrique Adoum or the theater of subversion* - Les cahiers du Littoral-Université Lille Nord, France.

Julio Pavanetti is a poet and a cultural activist. Founder and President of the international poets association 'Liceo Poético de Benidorm'. Honorary Vice President of the World Organization of Poets, Writers and Artists . Associate Academic at the North American Academy of Modern Literature. Director of the International Poetry Festival 'Benidorm & Costa Blanca'. Member of the Association of Spanish Writers and Artists and Spanish Collegiate Association of Writers. He had received many awards, honors and recognitions for his poetry and his cultural work. He has published eleven books and participated in more than 40 international anthologies. His poems have been translated into 14 languages.

Translator: María Juliana Villafañe is a poet, narrator, screenwriter, playwright and composer of popular music. She has published *Dimensiones en el amor* (Ramallo Brothers, 1992), awarded in New

York with the prize Palma Julia de Burgos, *Entre Dimensiones* (Isla Negra, Puerto Rico, 2002), *Aurora and her Intergalactic Journeys* (Planeta, 2003) and *Fly Without Wings* (Baquiana 2012). She won first place with the lyrics of the song *Live Today* at the III Ibero-american Festival of Puerto Rico and Argentina. Some of her poems and texts have been published in multiple anthologies in Argentina, Spain, the United States, Mexico, Peru, Brazil, Puerto Rico and Venezuela.

Liana Sakelliou studied English at the University of Athens (B.A.), Edinburgh (Grad Diploma), Essex (M.A.), and The Pennsylvania State University (Ph.D.). She is Professor in English and Chair of the Department of English Language and Literature at The University of Athens where she teaches Creative Writing and American Literature. Her 17 books with poems, scholarly articles, essays, and translations have been widely published in Greece, France and the U.S.A. She is a member of The Greek Authors' Society.

Lily Exarchopoulou is a writer. She has published three novels, one book of poetry and a Greek reader. Her latest novel was I on the short list of the Athens Prize for Literature. Her short stories have been published in anthologies, newspapers and literary magazines and one of her novels was the gist of the eponymous play staged in a prominent Athenian theater. She has translated from English into Greek works by world - acclaimed writers such as D.H. Lawrence, L. Durrell, E.Said, J.Berger et. al. She is a literary reviewer, columnist and has taught Greek and English Language and Literature as well as Ancient History in high schools and History of European Literature in the Greek Open University.

Lipi Da Mahandev is a young poet. He writes in Punjabi . There is a book of poetry to his credit. By profession he is a Hindi teacher in a government school. His poetry is about the miseries of a poor man. He also struggles for them in real life.

Maren Schönfeld, poetess and journalist. She has three poetry books published so far. In 2017 she received the Poetry Award from the Hamburg Writers' Association (Writers' Association Hamburg). **Translator:** Klaus-Dieter Wirth is a retired teacher of modern languages (German, English, French, Spanish, Dutch). He is a recognized international haiku expert. As an active member of 8 haiku societies (DE, AT, NL/BE, FR, ES, GB, US, JP) he has published hundreds of haiku and articles in journals and anthologies besides 2 individual multilingual books: *Zugvögel – Migratory Birds- Oiseaux migrateurs – Aves migratorias*, and *Im Sog der Stille – In the Wake of Silence – Au sillage du silence – En la estela del silencio*.

Meenu Sukhman is a young poetess. She writes in Punjabi. . There are two books to her credit. Her poetry is about women and life. She is also a good painter . By profession she is a Hindi Teacher in a government school.

Mesut Şenol graduated from the Political Science Faculty of Ankara University. His five poetry collections have been published and many of his poetry and literary translations have appeared in many national and foreign literary publications and anthologies. He has attended a number of national and international poetry and literary festivals both at home and abroad, and acted as an organizer for some of them. He has received numerous literary awards both at home and abroad. He is a member of many literary organizations. In May 2016, he was elected to serve on the Executive Board of the Three Seas (Baltic Sea, Black Sea and the Mediterranean Sea) Writers and Translators Council. He is the Turkish Cultural Delegate to the Liceo Poetico De Benidorm based in Spain.

Nurduran Duman is a Turkish poet who lives in Istanbul. Her books include *Yenilgi Oyunu*, the 2005 Cemal Sureya Poetry Award winner, and *Mi Bemol*. *Semi Circle*, a chapbook of her poems translated into English, was published in the United States in 2016 and in the UK in 2017 and further translations can be found in Modern Poetry in Translation (MPT), Asymptote Journal, Colorado Review, Faultline, Interim, and Eleven Eleven etc., journals. Her poems also have been translated into and published in Finnish, Bulgarian, Romanian, Slovak, French, German and Occitan. She is a member of the Turkish PEN.

Translator: Andrew Wessels currently splits his time between Los Angeles and Istanbul. He has held fellowships from Poets & Writers and the Black Mountain Institute. *Semi Circle*, a chapbook of his translations of the Turkish poet Nurduran Duman, was published by Goodmorning Menagerie in 2016. He is an editor at Les Figues Press and The Offending Adam. *A Turkish Dictionary*, published by 1913 Press, is his first book. His poems, translations, and collaborations can be found in VOLT, Witness, Fence, Tammy Journal, Faultline, and Colorado Review, among others.

Reimer Boy Eilers lives as a free lance author in Hamburg. He is the chairman of the German Writers' Guild in the State of Hamburg and a member of the German PEN Club. In 2017 he published his Collected Poems under the titel "Speaking with Tongues of the Sea".

Ruhsan Iskifoğlu completed her middle and high school education at Eastern Mediterranean College in 2001. In 2007, she graduated at Eastern Mediterranean University Faculty of Education. In 2008, she won a prize for her poetry entitled *Aranjues Mon Amour* in the contest between two societies of Turkish poetry. Between 2013 and 2016, she did poetry and panel translations for the international Cyprus İskele festival. Her poems have been published in magazines, her first book *Gözlemci Konuk Yazılı Kağıt Yayınları* in 2013, and her second book *Şeffaf Söküm Yasakmeyve Yayınları* in 2016

Surjit Singh Jeet is a senior poet and storywriter He is a retired accountant. There are two books to his credit. He writes in Punjabi and also in English.

Tariel Chanturia graduated from Tbilisi State University (faculty of philology, department of journalism) in 1956. His first poetry collection *Fleeing* was published in 1964. When he appeared on the literary scene, he attracted attention with his daring experiments, which were very much a form of fleeing. He often uses irony, parody, paradox, grotesqueries and slang. He has also published collections of children's verse, critical essays, translations, etc.

Tarsem is a poet and prose writer. He is a National Award - winning writer. There are 50 books to his credit. His writings are about the life of the common man and nature. He also writes for children. He is a Hindi teacher in a government school by profession.

Uwe Friesel, free lance writer in Salzwedel, Germany, has published novels, short stories, poems, children books and radio drama. His German translations of short stories by John Updike and novels by Vladimir Nabokov are noted. Major theatres have staged his new translation of Ben Jonson's Elisabethian play "Volpone". He was awarded a number of literary awards, like the prestigious Rome Prize Villa Massimo. President of the German Writers' Union from 1989 till 1994, at the time of German reunification. Member of international P.E.N.

Yiorgos Chouliaras is an award-winning Greek poet, fictioneer, and essayist whose poetry in English translation has been published in major periodicals, including *Harvard Review, The Iowa Review, Poetry, Ploughshares, and World Literature Today*, and in international anthologies such as *New European Poets*. The poem *Refugees* and his work in general has also been translated into Bulgarian, Croatian, French, French sign language, Irish, Japanese, Scots, Turkish, and other languages. He serves as President of the Hellenic Authors' Society.

Co-translator: David Mason is an award-winning American poet, librettist, and essayist, who has served as Poet Laureate of the State of Colorado.

Zorin Diaconescu, graduate of the English Language Department of the Faculty of Letters – Babes-Bolyai University, Cluj, Romania. Building a bridge between Romanian and English – a job for a lifetime. Occasionally, he writes poetry. He has also published a documentary book about the year 1989.